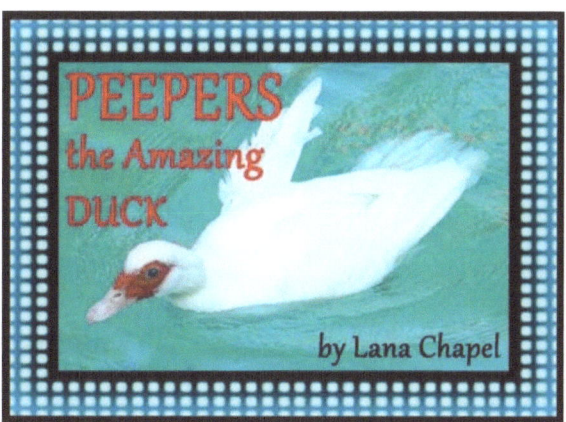

~ PEEPERS ~
the
Amazing Duck

by

Lana Chapel

Introduction

This is a true story about an injured baby Muscovy duck we took in and adopted. She became our "child" and shared our lives for 18 1/2 years! She was loved beyond compare!

In most places Muscovy ducks are considered to be nuisances and are captured by animal control to suffer a tragic fate...

In many places the all-white Muscovy ducks, like our Peepers, are raised as food in horrible conditions on commercial duck farms, where they are crammed together in cages to keep them from fighting and losing weight.

This book hopes to raise awareness about these intelligent and beautiful ducks. Most of the proceeds will go to various wildlife rescue organizations.

From the moment I first held her in my hands~~

That tiny, fuzzy duckling, all alone..

I seemed to know that God had special plans

For us to raise that "Angel" as our own.

She was wounded, she was fragile and afraid,

And confused by this new world to which she came.

But she calmed at the small peeping sounds I made-

Which she answered..and that's how she got her name.

So our bathtub soon became her private pond,

And her tiny feathers soon began to grow.

We formed a permanent and loving bond;

And though we tried, we couldn't let her go!

When it came to ducks, we hardly knew a thing!--

Though some lived at a lovely pond nearby.

When I took her there they broke her little wing;

Though it healed, she could never really fly.

As she grew we all went swimming and played ball!..

And we built a cozy cage for her inside

Filled with toy duckies, and she loved them all!

(She'd laid eggs that would not hatch--although she tried!)

(Peepers in the pool)

(Hello!..)

(Come on in!..)

(Peepers & her toys..)

(Sleepy "Peepy")

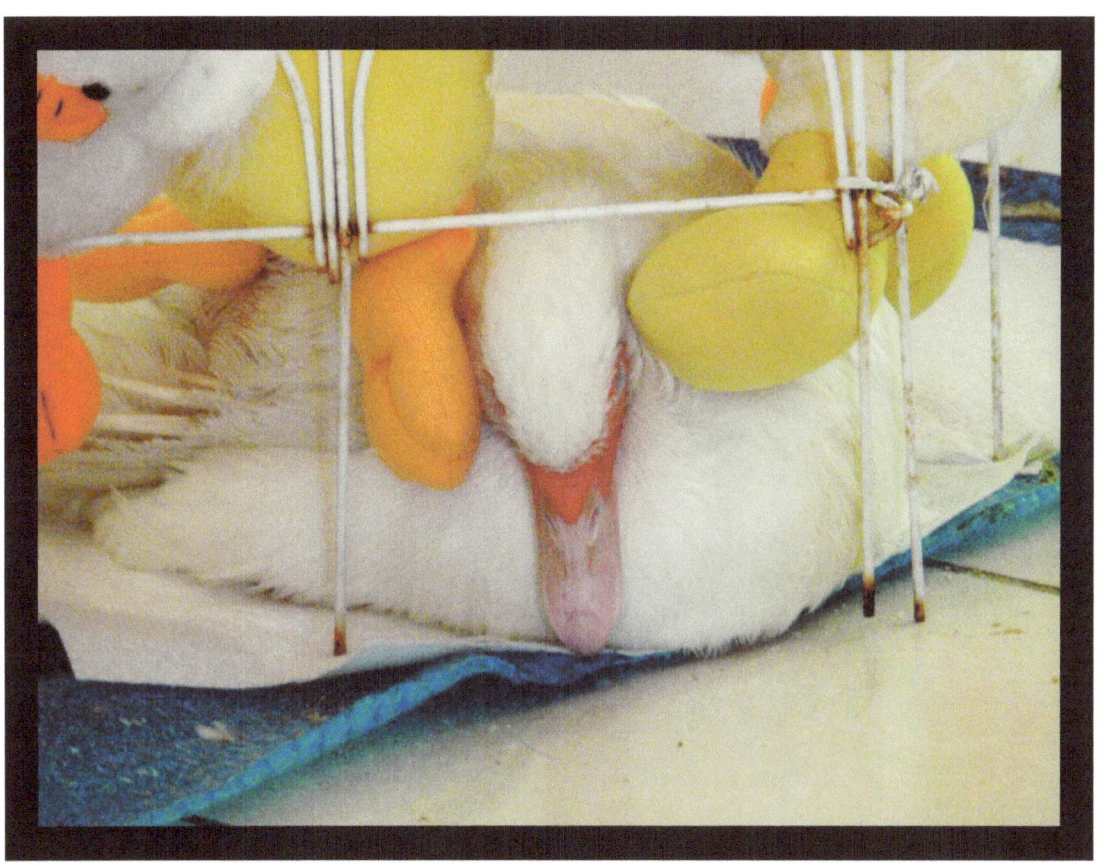

She loved to look in mirrors day and night!

She thought that her reflection was her mate!

And she loved for us to kiss and hug her tight..

And run up to us as though she couldn't wait!

(Peepers & Mommy Lana & Daddy Mark)

Each morning she peeped really loud for me

To come so she could step onto my hand!

Then at the door she handed me the key!--

And looked at me like, "Don't you understand?"

She wore a diaper made of plastic wrap
So she could wander freely through the house.
Of course sometimes she'd have a small mishap,
Which never failed to raise a few eyebrows!

She loved to hear my music when I played

And sometimes she would even peep along.

Her favorite food was pizza I'm afraid...

Which made it good to keep her diaper on!

She loved to wear some anklets, just like me--

So I made her a pretty one to wear.

She'd stick her little webbed foot out for she

Wanted everyone to see it there!

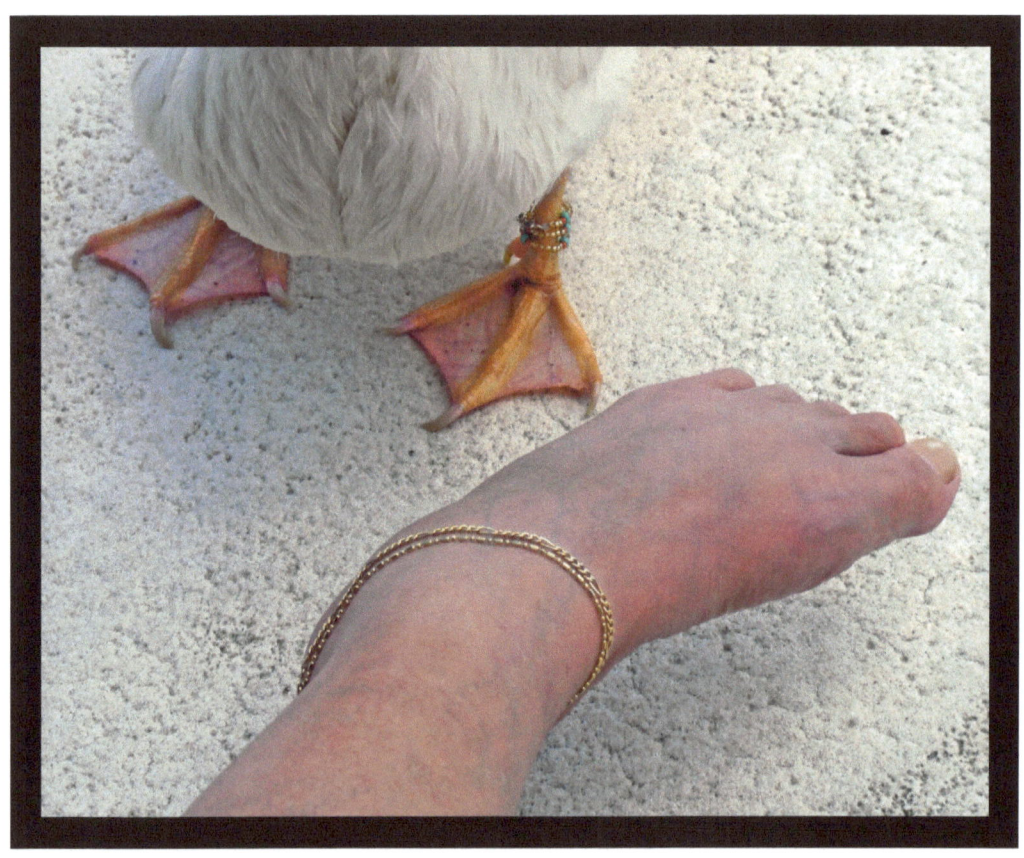

(Pretty Peepers!)

On holidays she was a huge surprise..
At Christmas she helped decorate the tree!

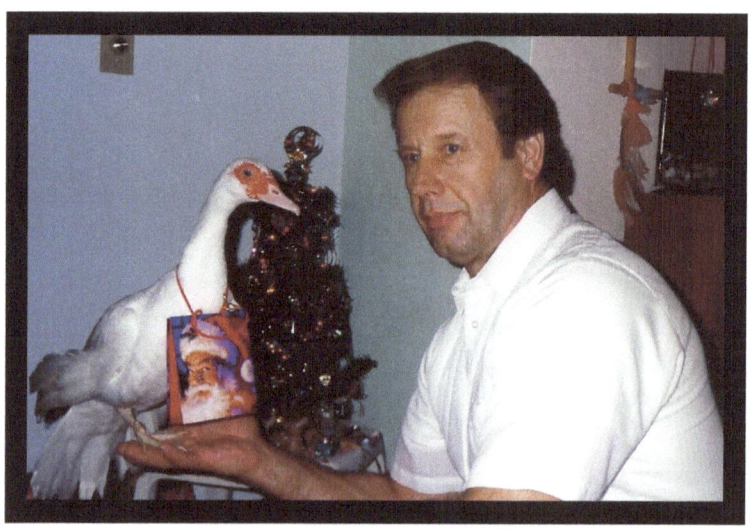

(Christmas with Peepers & Bo)

And Easter-time was awesome in my eyes,
For the great big Easter eggs she laid for me!!

Each time someone would ask if we had kids.
We'd never hesitate to answer back!
We'd say we had a daughter--for we DID!--
And though she couldn't talk, she sure could quack!

Then we would laugh and finish our reply--
About her "furry" brother we called Bo!
And pretty soon they'd figure out just why
We bragged about our "Critter Children" so!

Yes, she became a very loving part

Of our lives for over eighteen years!

The day she went to Heaven broke our hearts...

But amazing memories sparkle through our tears.

Though we *still* find it's hard to let her go,

And though we mourn and grieve, and often cry..

One thought brings us comfort, for we know

Our little Angel finally can fly!

The End

Lana Chapel

Lana Chapel became a professional singer/songwriter/performer at the age of 11, with her first songs published by major Nashville publishers: Owen Bradley and by Tree Music. She had songs published by 4 Star Music at age 14, and was a staff songwriter with Vintage Music, Combine Music, 4 Star Music, Frank & Nancy Music, First Lady Music, Richey Music Group, and MetroCountry Music. Her songs have been recorded by: Eddy Arnold, Henson Cargill, Tompall Glaser, Lee Hazelwood, Lester Flatt, Nancy Sinatra and various other new and Independent artists.

Lana's was a recording artist for Monument Records, Dot Records and Mega Records throughout her teens and early 20's. She was produced and managed by Bob Tubert, Fred Foster, Bergen White, Dennis Linde, and Kris Kristofferson.

As a young girl Lana dreamed of creating stories in more than just songs. She is self-taught in all her skills and is also a scriptwriter, poet, Illustrator, narrator, musician, among other things, and has recently made her debut as a childrens' book author. She does all the illustrations, songs and music to accompany her books.

For more history and information about Lana visit her website: www.lanachapel.com , and Lana Chapel on FaceBook, and YouTube.

www.ingramcontent.com/pod-product-compliance
Lightning Source LLC
Chambersburg PA
CBHW060814290526
45792CB00005BA/1654